W9-DBQ-566

LAURENCE DUNN

British Passenger Liners

ADLARD COLES LIMITED · SOUTHAMPTON
IN ASSOCIATION WITH
GEORGE G. HARRAP & CO LTD
LONDON · TORONTO · WELLINGTON · SYDNEY
AND
JOHN DE GRAFF INC.
NEW YORK

Printed and bound in Great Britain
by Hazell Watson & Viney Limited
Aylesbury and Slough

FOREWORD

VERY rare indeed is the individual whose interest and imagination is not quickened by the sight of a ship. Differing essentially from cars and aircraft, which are but mass produced, every vessel has an individuality and character of her own. More particularly does this apply to the passenger liner, which of all types surely has the widest appeal.

She must of necessity be far more than just a safe and seaworthy vehicle for the carriage of passengers and cargo; she must also provide all the amenities and service of a modern hotel, together with maximum opportunities for relaxation and enjoyment. Each ship at sea is as self-sufficient as a city; and no two are alike. This last point is borne out by the speed and performance of sisterships, which in some instances show surprising variations even though built to a common design.

The aim of this book—which I hope may further this interest—is to give a concise description of every deep-sea passenger liner owned in Great Britain, so presented that it will not only provide quick reference to each individual vessel, but also afford easy comparison between ships of a fleet. The companies are arranged alphabetically, their passenger-carrying ships (those with accommodation for over twelve) in order of relative importance. Thus, with text and illustration side by side, evolution in design becomes the more easy to see. It is complete to a minimum of 6,000 tons gross, besides including a number of smaller size ships. Certain Commonwealth vessels operating overseas are not included however, as these will feature in a later work.

As the result of periodic refits many items – such as number of passengers carried and tonnage – change with the years. Details of route, passenger capacity, service speed (and in most cases tonnage) have been supplied by the owners; while reliance has also been placed on that most important of all shipping reference books – *Lloyd's Register*.

Of the figures given, the length (overall) and breadth are to the nearest foot, draught to the nearest inch. Although the normal routes are shown, it will be remembered that many liners are periodically used for cruising. As regards machinery, it is only necessary to make the following points: that for turbine driven ships, where the letters S.R. (single reduction gearing) and D.R. (double reduction) are omitted, a combination of both types of gearing is used. With motorships the type of diesel engine fitted is given, as being of more interest than the name of the manufacturer. In fact, for nearly all liners, the ship builder has also been responsible for the machinery.

Finally I must express my grateful thanks to the many whose kind co-operation has made this book possible, to the owners individually and to *Lloyd's Register of Shipping*, to G. A. Game, Esq., and others, and to my friends Keith P. Lewis and R. M. Scott for their especial contributions.

LAURENCE DUNN

NOTE: An asterisk ⋆ by ship's name denotes illustration.

ANCHOR LINE LTD., Glasgow

CALEDONIA, CILICIA, CIRCASSIA*

Route: U.K. to India and Pakistan (Liverpool, Port Said, Aden, Karachi, and Bombay). *Built:* 1948, 1938, 1937 by Fairfield, Glasgow. *Gross tonnage:* 11,252; 11,172; 11,170. *D.W. tonnage:* 10,417; 10,287; 10,287. *Dimensions:* 506 ft × 66 ft. *Draught:* 27 ft 6 ins. *Engines:* Doxford type diesels. Twin screw. *Speed:* 16 knots. *Passengers:* (first class) CALEDONIA 304 adults, 22 children. Other ships: 298 adults, 22 children. Partial air-conditioning. The CIRCASSIA was the Company's first motorship. During the last war she served first as an A.M.C. Later, as a troopship, she took part in the landings at Salerno, St Tropez, and the Straits of Malacca. CILICIA served as an A.M.C. for 4½ years, then as a troopship.

BIBBY LINE LTD., Liverpool

DERBYSHIRE*

Route: Liverpool, Port Said, Port Sudan, Aden, Colombo, Rangoon. *Built:* 1935 by Fairfield, Glasgow. *Tonnage:* 10,641 gross. 10,328 d.w. *Dimensions:* 501 ft × 66 ft. *Draught:* 29 ft 3 ins. *Engines:* Sulzer type diesels. Twin screw. *Speed:* 14½ knots. *Passengers:* 115 first. The last of a group of five four-masted motor liners built 1926–35 for the Company's Burma trade, the DERBYSHIRE entered service in November 1935. During the war she served first as an A.M.C., then as a transport. Like STAFFORDSHIRE and WORCESTERSHIRE, was given 'new look' during her post-war reconstruction.

STAFFORDSHIRE, WORCESTERSHIRE*

Route: Liverpool, Port Said, Port Sudan, Aden, Colombo, Rangoon. *Built:* 1929, 1931 by Fairfield, Glasgow. *Tonnage:* 10,018/10,329 gross. 10,400/10,237 d.w. *Dimensions:* 500/501 ft × 62/64 ft. *Draught:* 29 ft 1 in./ 29 ft 3 ins. *Engines:* Sulzer type diesels. Twin screw. *Speed:* 14½ knots. *Passengers:* 109/115 first. As built they had four masts and one tall thin funnel. STAFFORDSHIRE used as trooper January 1942 – November 1948. WORCESTERSHIRE as an A.M.C. was torpedoed N. of Ireland early in war. Towed home and started as troopship 1943; present at D-day and Malaya landings. Upper-works cut down and after-well lengthened during post-war refit. STAFFORDSHIRE has lifeboats one deck lower.

4

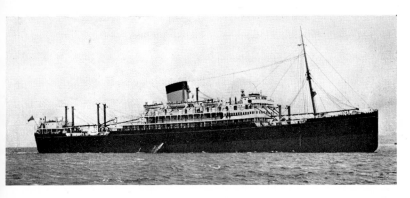

BIBBY LINE LTD., Liverpool (*contd.*)

WARWICKSHIRE, LEICESTERSHIRE★

Route: Liverpool, Port Said, Port Sudan, Aden, Colombo, Rangoon. *Built:* 1948, 1949 by Fairfield, Glasgow. *Tonnage:* 8,917/8,922 gross. 9,589/9,614 d.w. *Dimensions:* 498 ft × 60 ft. *Draught:* 27 ft 6 ins. *Engines:* D.R. geared turbines. Single screw. *Speed:* 14½ knots. *Passengers:* 76 first. The Company's first post-war passenger ships, and their first for very many years to be turbine driven. WARWICKSHIRE, the earlier of the pair, lacks the LEICESTERSHIRE'S last pair of derrick posts and in their place has a tall mainmast.

Troopship:

OXFORDSHIRE★

Route: Government troop-carrying. *Built:* 1957 by Fairfield, Glasgow. *Tonnage:* 20,586 gross. 7,300 d.w. *Dimensions:* 609 ft × 78 ft. *Draught:* 26 ft 5 ins. *Engines:* D.R. geared turbines. Twin screw. *Speed:* 17 knots. *Passengers:* 220 first, 100 second, 180 third, 1,000 troops. Stabilisers. Hospital spaces air-conditioned. Britain's second post-war troopship, the OXFORDSHIRE ran trials in February 1957 and attained a mean speed of 21 knots. Almost twice the size of any previous Bibby ship, she is generally similar to the earlier but two-masted NEVASA.

Troopship:

DEVONSHIRE★

Route: Government troop-carrying. *Built:* 1939 by Fairfield, Glasgow. *Tonnage:* 12,773 gross. 3,497 d.w. *Dimensions:* 517 ft × 63 ft. *Draught:* 24 ft 7 ins. *Engines:* Sulzer type diesels. Twin screw. *Speed:* 13½ knots. *Passengers:* 130 first, 96 second, 99 third (includes permanent staff), 824 troops. One of four generally similar pre-war troopships, others being British India Line's DILWARA and DUNERA and P. & O.'s ETTRICK (sunk November 1942). Like the first named, her original forward well deck was built up during her 1953 major refit, when three-tier standees were fitted in place of former hammocks.

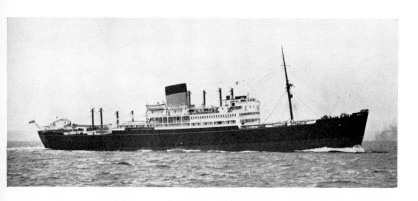

BLUE FUNNEL LINE, Liverpool (Alfred Holt & Co.)

HELENUS, JASON, HECTOR,* IXION

Route: U.K. – Australia (Liverpool, Port Said, Aden, Albany/Fremantle, Adelaide, Melbourne, Sydney). *Built:* 1949, 1950, 1950, 1951 by Harland & Wolff. (JASON by Swan Hunter.) *Tonnage:* 10,129/10,160/10,125/10,125 gross. Approx. 11,300 d.w. *Dimensions:* 523 ft × 69 ft. *Draught:* 31 ft. *Engines:* D.R. geared turbines. Single Screw. *Speed:* 18¼ knots. *Passengers:* Approx. 30 first. HELENUS, the first of the quartette, ran trials in October 1949. In layout this group differs slightly from rather smaller P class (Far Eastern trade) in having extra (4th) hatch forward.

PELEUS, PYRRHUS, PATROCLUS, PERSEUS*

Route: Liverpool, Rotterdam, Port Said, Singapore, Hong Kong, Japan, (Colombo homewards). *Built:* First two 1949 by Cammell Laird, others 1950 by Vickers-Armstrongs, Newcastle. *Tonnage:* First two 10,093, others 10,109 gross. Approx. 11,200 d.w. *Dimensions:* 516 ft × 68 ft. *Draught:* 30 ft 8 ins. *Engines:* D.R. geared turbines. Single screw. *Speed:* 18½ knots. *Passengers:* Approx. 30 first. All bear traditional Company names. The previous PATROCLUS, built 1923, 11,314 tons gross, was sunk in November 1940 while acting as an Armed Merchant Cruiser.

CHARON*

Route: Singapore–Fremantle. *Built:* 1936 by Caledon, Dundee. *Tonnage:* 3,964 gross. 3,060 d.w. *Dimensions:* 336 ft × 51 ft. *Draught:* 20 ft 8 ins. *Engines:* B. & W. type diesels. Single Screw. *Speed:* 13½ knots. *Passengers:* 88. Similar ship GORGON operates on same route. Both given a major refit late 1958. An unusual feature of this trade, for which they were designed, is that at some of the Australian ports visited the tides are such that at low water the ships are left high and dry on the sand.

BLUE FUNNEL LINE, Liverpool (Alfred Holt & Co.) (*contd.*)

GORGON*

Route: Singapore–Fremantle. *Built:* 1933 by Caledon, Dundee. *Tonnage:* 3,678 gross. 3,125 d.w. *Dimensions:* 336 ft × 51 ft. *Draught:* 20 ft 7 ins. *Engines:* B. & W. type diesel. Single screw. *Speed:* 13½ knots. *Passengers:* 72. Generally similar to CHARON on previous page (*q.v.*).

GUNUNG DJATI,* (ex Empire Orwell 1958, ex Empire Doon 1949, ex Pretoria 1945)

Route: Indonesia–Jeddah, with pilgrims. *Built:* 1936 by Blohm & Voss, Hamburg. *Tonnage:* 18,036 gross. *Dimensions:* 577 ft × 72 ft. *Draught:* 25 ft 1 in. *Engines:* S.R. geared turbines. Twin screw. *Speed:* 16 knots. *Passengers:* 106 pilgrims in first class (including 2 luxury suites), 2,000 in lower-grade quarters. Built for Deutsche Ost – Afrika Linie. (Sister WINDHUK, now U.S.S. LEJEUNE.) As trooper managed by Orient Line, chartered 1958 by Pan-Islamic S.S. Co. Karachi, as pilgrim ship. Bought by Blue Funnel November 1958 and given Clyde refit. Left Liverpool March 1959 for Far East where she is based.

BLUE STAR LINE LTD., London

ARGENTINA STAR, BRASIL STAR, URUGUAY STAR, PARAGUAY STAR*

Route U.K.–S. America. (Ports: London, Lisbon, Madeira, Las Palmas, Teneriffe, Recife, Salvador, Rio de Janeiro, Santos, Montevideo, Buenos Aires.) *Built:* 1947, 1947, 1948, 1948, by Cammell Laird. *Tonnage:* First two 10,716 gross. Others 10,723; 10,722. 11,600 d.w. *Dimensions:* 503 ft × 68 ft. *Draught:* approx. 31 ft 1 in. *Engines:* D.R. geared turbines. Single screw. *Speed:* 16 knots. *Passengers:* ARGENTINA 51 first, plus Pullmans. Others 53 first, plus Pullmans. The first British liners to have engines so far aft, they have been continuously employed on the above service, sailing at two – three weekly intervals. Large refrigerated cargo space. The first pair have shorter funnels, also derrick posts by mast.

11

BOOTH LINE, Liverpool (The Booth Steamship Co. Ltd.)

HUBERT*

Route: U.K. and Portugal, Madeira, British West Indies, and River Amazon. (Liverpool, Leixoes, Lisbon, Madeira, Barbados, Trinidad, Belem, and Manaus.) *Built:* 1955 by Cammell Laird, Birkenhead. *Tonnage:* 7,905 gross. 6,347 d.w. *Dimensions:* 439 ft × 60 ft. *Draught:* 25 ft 4 ins. *Engines:* D.R. geared turbines. Single screw. *Speed:* 15 knots. *Passengers:* 74 first, 96 tourist. Few passenger liners have their machinery so far aft. In this the Booth Line followed the lead set by the parent firm, the Blue Star Line, for the latter's four passenger ships (*q.v.*).

HILARY*

Route: U.K. and Portugal, Madeira, British West Indies, and River Amazon. (Liverpool, Leixoes, Lisbon, Madeira, Barbados, Trinidad Belem, and Manaus.) *Built:* 1931 by Cammell Laird, Birkenhead. *Tonnage:* 7,392 gross. 5,611 d.w. *Dimensions:* 442 ft × 56 ft. *Draught:* 24 ft 8 ins. *Engines:* Trip. exp. and exhaust L.P. turbine. Single screw. *Speed:* 14½ knots. Passengers: 86 first, 122 tourist. During the early part of the war the HILARY was used as an Ocean Boarding Vessel and later, from 1943, as an H.Q. ship in Combined Operations. As such she was at the Salerno and Normandy landings, during the latter as flagship, Force 'J'.

BRITISH INDIA S. NAV. CO. LTD.

KENYA*

Route: U.K.–East Africa (London, Gibraltar/Malta, Port Said, Aden, Mombasa, Tanga, Zanzibar, Dar-es-Salaam, Beira. Homeward also Marseilles and Gibraltar). *Built:* 1951 by Barclay Curle, Glasgow. *Tonnage:* 14,464 gross. 9,720 d.w. *Dimensions:* 540 ft × 71 ft. *Draught:* 27 ft 6 ins. *Engines:* S.R. geared turbines. Twin screw. *Speed:* 16 knots. *Passengers:* 194 first, 103 tourist. Air-conditioning in some public rooms. When built, the KENYA and UGANDA were the largest yet owned by the B.I. White hull adopted 1955 as on their other passenger ships. The previous KENYA – built 1930 for the India – E. African run – still operates as Sitmar Line's CASTEL FELICE.

BRITISH INDIA S. NAV. CO. LTD. (*contd.*)

UGANDA*

Route: U.K. – East Africa (ports as KENYA above). *Built:* 1952 by Barclay Curle, Glasgow. *Tonnage:* 14,430 gross. 9,630 d.w. *Dimensions:* 540 ft × 71 ft. *Draught:* 27 ft 6 ins. *Engines:* S.R. geared turbines. Twin screw. *Speed:* 16 knots. *Passengers:* 167 first, 133 tourist. Partial air-conditioning. Delivered a year after the KENYA, the UGANDA has slightly different internal arrangements and a funnel 12 ft taller. The 450th ship to be built for the B.I. since its formation in 1856, she attained 19.25 knots on trial. First sailing 2 August, 1952.

KAMPALA, KARANJA*

Route: Bombay – Africa, extending to Durban. *Built:* 1947, 1948 by A. Stephen, Glasgow. *Tonnage:* 10,304/10,294 gross. 9,135/9,120 d.w. *Dimensions:* 507 ft × 66 ft. *Draught:* 27 ft 3 ins. *Engines:* S.R. geared turbines. Twin screw. *Speed:* 16 knots. *Passengers:* KAMPALA 60 first, 180 second; KARANJA 60 first, 180 second, 75 third. These ships also carry over 800 unberthed passengers. Launched respectively on 10 December, 1946 and 10 March 1948, they replaced an earlier pair KARANJA and KENYA, built for this service in 1930–31. This earlier KARANJA was sunk as an assault ship during the N. African landings November 1942.

AMRA,* ARONDA

Route: AMRA: Bombay – Africa (as far as Dar-es-Salaam); ARONDA: Karachi – Chittagong via Colombo. *Built:* 1938, 1941 by Swan Hunter & W. R., Newcastle. *Tonnage:* 8,314/8,396 gross. 6,150/4,791 d.w. *Dimensions:* 461 ft × 61 ft. *Draught:* 23 ft 9 ins. *Engines:* S.R. geared turbines. Twin screw. *Speed:* 16½ knots. *Passengers:* AMRA: 58 'A' Grade, 164 'B' Grade. ARONDA: 44 first, 22 second, plus 28 interchangeable, 60 inter-mediate. These two also carry some 700 and 1,800 unberthed passengers. A third vessel of this class, the ASKA (Swan Hunter, 1939) was torpedoed off Ireland in September 1940. AMRA saw war service as a hospital ship.

BRITISH INDIA S. NAV. CO. LTD. (contd.)

MOMBASA*

Route: Mombasa – Mtwara via intermediate ports. *Built:* 1950 by Henry Robb, Leith. *Tonnage:* 2,213 gross. 1,364 d.w. *Dimensions:* 266 ft × 43 ft. *Draught:* 14 ft 6 ins. *Engines:* Polar type diesels. Twin screw. *Speed:* 12 knots. *Passengers:* 8 first, 16 second, 250 deck. Engaged on local feeder service. Experimental use of white hull discontinued in favour of that shown.

Troopship:

NEVASA*

Route: Government troop-carrying. *Built:* 1956 by Barclay Curle, Glasgow. *Tonnage:* 20,527 gross. *Dimensions:* 609 ft × 78 ft. *Draught:* 26 ft 7 ins. *Engines:* D.R. geared turbines. Twin screw. *Speed:* 17 knots. *Passengers:* 220 first, 100 second, 180 third, 1,000 troops. Stabilisers. Hospital spaces air-conditioned. The NEVASA was delivered in July 1956 – the Company's Centenary year. Notable in being the first to be designed solely for trooping, and the first troopship to be given stabilisers. First class, 1, 2, or 3 berth; second 2, 3, or 4 berth; third 3 or 4 berth. Troops in standee berths. Followed by generally similar OXFORDSHIRE.

Troopships:

DILWARA,* DUNERA

Route: Government troop-carrying. *Built:* 1936, 1937 by Barclay Curle, Glasgow. *Tonnage:* 12,555/12,615 gross. 3,775/3,657 d.w. *Dimensions:* 517 ft × 63 ft. *Draught:* 25 ft. *Engines:* Doxford type diesels. Twin screw. *Speed:* 14 knots. *Passengers:* DILWARA: 125 first, 96 second, 104 third, 705 troops; DUNERA: 123 first, 95 second, 100 third, 835 troops. After war-time service – when troop capacity was raised to over 2,300 – both were given a major refit to meet new peace-time standards, with three-tier standee berths fitted for troops. Original well deck forward built up at same time.

CANADIAN PACIFIC RLY. CO.

Managers: Canadian Pacific Steamships Ltd., Liverpool

EMPRESS OF —— (Not yet named)

Route: Summer: Liverpool to Quebec and Montreal. Winter: Cruising. *Building:* by Vickers-Armstrongs, Newcastle. *Tonnage:* 27,500 gross. 9,000 d.w. *Dimensions:* 650 ft × 86 ft 6 ins. *Draught:* 29 ft. *Engines:* D.R. geared turbines. Twin screw. *Speed:* 21 knots. *Passengers:* 200 first, about 860 tourist. Fully air-conditioned. The biggest passenger liner to be built on the Tyne for 50 years, it is estimated that she will cost 23 million Canadian dollars. Keel laid 27 January 1959. Special features include stabilisers and bulbous bow.

EMPRESS OF BRITAIN★

Route: Summer: Liverpool to Quebec and Montreal. Winter: (December – March) to St John, N.B. *Built:* 1956 by Fairfield, Glasgow. *Tonnage:* 25,516 gross. Approx. 9,000 d.w. *Dimensions:* 640 ft × 85 ft. *Draught:* 29 ft. *Engines:* D.R. geared turbines. Twin screw. *Speed:* 20 knots. *Passengers:* 160 first, 894 tourist. Stabilisers. Fully air-conditioned. The first ship built in Great Britain to be completely air-conditioned. Launched on 22 June 1955 and named by H.M. the Queen. Six cargo holds, with approx. one-fifth of this space insulated.

EMPRESS OF ENGLAND★

Route: Summer: Liverpool to Quebec and Montreal. Winter: Liverpool to St John, N.B. *Built:* 1957 by Vickers-Armstrongs, Newcastle. *Tonnage:* 25,585 gross. 8,910 d.w. *Dimensions:* 640 ft × 85 ft. *Draught:* 29 ft. *Engines:* D.R. geared turbines. Twin screw. *Speed:* 20 knots. *Passengers:* 160 first, 898 tourist. Stabilisers. Fully air-conditioned. Launched by Lady Eden on 9 May 1956. Ready almost exactly a year after the EMPRESS OF BRITAIN, her maiden voyage started on 18 April 1957. In all major respects the two ships are identical, differences being confined to detail such as decoration and layout of public rooms, and externally to bridge, etc.

CANADIAN PACIFIC RLY. CO. (*contd.*)

EMPRESS OF FRANCE★ (ex Duchess of Bedford 1948)

Route: Summer: Liverpool to Quebec and Montreal. Winter: Liverpool to St John, N.B. *Built:* 1928 by John Brown, Clydebank. *Tonnage:* 20,448 gross. 9,382 d.w. *Dimensions:* 601 ft × 75 ft. *Draught:* 27 ft 7 ins. *Engines:* S.R. geared turbines. Twin screw. *Speed:* 18 knots. *Passengers:* 218 first, 482 tourist. Launched on 1 June 1928 as the first of four DUCHESS cabin-class ships. Served as a troopship from August 1939 to February 1947. Reconditioned and renamed, she made her first post-war voyage 1 September 1948. Given a complete refit winter 1958–9, also 'new look' tapered funnels.

CUNARD LINE (The Cunard Steam-Ship Co. Ltd.)

QUEEN ELIZABETH★

Route: Southampton – Cherbourg – New York. *Built:* 1940 by John Brown, Clydebank. *Tonnage:* 83,673 gross. 16,881 d.w. *Dimensions:* 1,031 ft × 119 ft. *Draught:* 39 ft 6 ins. *Engines:* S.R. geared turbines. Four screws. *Speed:* 28½ knots. *Passengers:* 790 first, 657 cabin, 793 tourist. Two sets of stabilisers. Public rooms air-conditioned. Launched on 27 September 1938, she made a secret maiden voyage to New York in March 1940. From April 1941 until March 1946 she saw world-wide service, carrying over 800,000 passengers. It was not until 16 October 1946 that she sailed from Southampton on her first peace-time voyage.

QUEEN MARY★

Route: Southampton – Cherbourg – New York. *Built:* 1936 by John Brown, Clydebank. *Tonnage:* 81,237 gross. 17,000 d.w. *Dimensions:* 1,019 ft × 119 ft. *Draught:* 39 ft 4 ins. *Engines:* S.R. geared turbines. Four screws. *Speed:* 28½ knots. *Passengers:* 704 first, 740 cabin, 582 tourist. Two sets of stabilisers. Public-rooms air conditioned. Launched by Queen Mary on 26 September 1934, the QUEEN MARY entered service in May 1936. Able to carry over 10,500 men at a time, she proved invaluable as a troopship and in this role saw world-wide service. Her first post-war sailing from Southampton was in July 1947. In 1938 she averaged 30·99 knots Westwards (Bishop to Ambrose) and 31·69 knots Eastwards.

CUNARD LINE (The Cunard Steam-Ship Co. Ltd.) *(contd.)*

MAURETANIA*

Route: Southampton – Havre – Cobh – New York. *Built:* 1939 by Cammell Laird, Birkenhead. *Tonnage:* 35,655 gross. 9,178 d.w. *Dimensions:* 772 ft × 89 ft. *Draught:* 30 ft 10 ins. *Engines:* S.R. geared turbines. Twin screws. *Speed:* 23 knots. *Passengers:* 475 first, 368 cabin, 304 tourist. Fully air-conditioned. Launched on 28 July 1938, the MAURETANIA made only two round trips to America before war was declared. In 1940 she was converted into a troopship and continued as such until her release in September 1946. She resumed her Cunard sailings in April 1947.

CARONIA*

Route: Cruising most of the year. Occasional voyages Southampton – Havre – New York. *Built:* 1948 by John Brown, Clydebank. *Tonnage:* 34,172 gross. 7,921 d.w. *Dimensions:* 715 ft × 91 ft. *Draught:* 31 ft 7 ins. *Engines:* Geared turbines. Twin screw. *Speed:* 22 knots. *Passengers:* 582 first, 353 tourist. (One class only when cruising.) Fully air-conditioned. Named after a 20,000 ton two-funnelled liner built at the same yard in 1905, the present CARONIA was launched on 30 October 1947 by the Queen (then Princess Elizabeth). Entered service January 1949. Famous for her elaborate long distance dollar-earning cruises. Ship painted in three shades of green.

BRITANNIC*

Route: Liverpool – Cobh – New York. *Built:* 1930 by Harland & Wolff. *Tonnage:* 27,778 gross. 13,240 d.w. *Dimensions:* 712 ft × 82 ft. *Draught:* 35 ft. *Engines:* B. & W. type diesels. Twin screw. *Speed:* 17½ knots. *Passengers:* 369 first, 608 tourist. Now the world's largest motor liner (CAPETOWN CASTLE longer, but of less tonnage). Built for White Star Line's Liverpool – New York service. Maiden voyage June 1930. Despite merger with Cunard in 1934, has kept original funnel colour. As built, carried 1,550 passengers in three classes but after war-time trooping made into two class ship. Resumed old service May 1948.

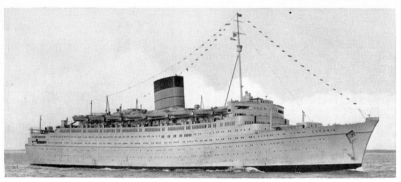

CUNARD LINE (The Cunard Steam-Ship Co. Ltd.) (*contd.*)

SAXONIA, IVERNIA, CARINTHIA, SYLVANIA★

Route: First two London/Southampton and Havre – Quebec and Montreal, or Halifax and New York. (Frequently Cobh also.) Others, Liverpool and Greenock – Quebec and Montreal, or Liverpool and Cobh – Halifax and New York. *Built:* 1954, 1955, 1956, 1957 by John Brown, Clydebank. *Tonnage:* 21,637/21,716/21,947/21,989 gross. Approx. 9,300/9,700 d.w. *Dimensions:* 608 ft × 80 ft. *Draught:* approx. 28 ft 7 ins. *Engines:* D.R. geared turbines. Twin screw. *Speed:* 19½ knots. *Passengers:* 110 first/819 tourist, 110/833, 154/714, and 154/724. Stabilisers. Public rooms air-conditioned. These, the largest Cunarders yet built for the Canadian trade, replace the six 14,000 ton 'A' class ships of the 'twenties.

MEDIA, PARTHIA★

Route: Liverpool – New York. *Built:* 1947 by John Brown. 1948 by Harland & Wolff. *Tonnage:* 13,345/13,362 gross. 11,636/11,516 d.w. *Dimensions:* 531 ft × 70 ft. *Draught:* 30 ft 2 ins. *Engines:* D.R. geared turbines. Twin screw. *Speed:* 18 knots. *Passengers:* 251 first. Stabilisers. Public rooms air-conditioned. PARTHIA, the first Cunarder to be built by Harland & Wolff. MEDIA, the first transatlantic liner to be given stabilisers. Entered service August 1947 and April 1948 respectively. The two maintain fortnightly sailings.

DONALDSON LINE, LTD., Glasgow

LAURENTIA★ (ex Medina Victory 1947), LISMORIA (ex Taos Victory 1948)

Route: Summer: Glasgow direct to Montreal. Winter: Glasgow direct to St John, N.B., and Halifax, N.S. *Built:* 1945 by Permanente (Shipyard No. 1) Richmond, California; 1945 by California S.B. Corp., Los Angeles. *Tonnage:* 8,349/8,323 gross. 10,160/10,309 d.w. *Dimensions:* 455 ft × 62 ft. *Draught:* 28 ft 7 ins. *Engines:* D.R. geared turbines. Single screw. *Speed:* 15 knots. *Passengers:* 55 first. Air-conditioning. After war-time service as U.S. troopers, both transferred to Britain, summer 1946. Managed respectively by Donaldson and Furness Withy until bought by Donaldson Line 1947. Then reconditioned for present trade.

DONALDSON LINE, LTD., Glasgow (*contd.*)

Managed for Ministry of Transport

CAPTAIN COOK,★ ex (Empire Brent 1951, ex Letitia 1946)

Route: Outwards, with emigrants, from Glasgow to New Zealand direct, via Panama. Homewards, she sometimes carries troops from Far East, etc. *Built:* 1925 by Fairfield, Glasgow. *Tonnage:* 13,876 gross. 8,481 d.w. *Dimensions:* 538 ft × 66 ft. *Draught:* 27 ft 8 ins. *Engines:* D.R. geared turbines. Twin screw. *Speed:* 14½ knots. *Passengers:* 1,050 one class. With sister ATHENIA (torpedoed 1939) was designed for the Anchor-Donaldson Line's Glasgow – Canada service. For some years has been chartered by the New Zealand Government to take settlers to that country under free passage scheme. This charter expires 1959.

ELDER DEMPSTER LINES LTD., Liverpool

AUREOL★

Route: Liverpool, Las Palmas, Freetown, Takoradi and Lagos (and vice-versa). *Built:* 1951 by A. Stephen, Glasgow. *Tonnage:* 14,083 gross. 7,025 d.w. *Dimensions:* 537 ft × 70 ft. *Draught:* 25 ft 1 in. *Engines:* Doxford type diesels. Twin screw. *Speed:* 16 knots. *Passengers:* 253 first plus 42 cots, 76 cabin, 24 interchangeable. The flagship of the line, the AUREOL ran trials in October 1951. She and the slightly smaller ACCRA and APAPA maintain a fortnightly service from Liverpool.

ACCRA, APAPA★

Route: Liverpool, Freetown, Takoradi, Lagos and vice-versa. ACCRA also calls at Las Palmas. APAPA also calls at Bathurst. *Built:* 1947, 1948, by Vickers-Armstrongs, Barrow. *Tonnage:* 11,599/11,607 gross. Both 6,982 d.w. *Dimensions:* 471 ft × 66 ft. *Draught:* 25 ft 6 ins. *Engines:* Doxford type diesels. Twin screw. *Speed:* 15½ knots. *Passengers:* 259 first plus 30 cots, 24 third. Delivered in September 1947 and March 1948 respectively, they perpetuate the names of an earlier pair. These, built in 1926 and of 9,300 tons, were sunk in July and October of 1940.

ELDER DEMPSTER LINES LTD., Liverpool (*contd.*)

CALABAR* (ex Umtali 1957), WINNEBA (ex Umgeni 1957)

Route: London, Madeira, Freetown, Takoradi, Lagos (and vice-versa). *Built:* 1936, 1938, by Swan Hunter & Wigham Richardson, Newcastle. *Tonnage:* 8,305/8,355 gross. 8,020/8,050 d.w. *Dimensions:* 468 ft × 61 ft. *Draught:* 25 ft 6 ins. *Engines:* Triple exp. L.P. exhaust turbines. Twin screw. *Speed:* 13½ knots. *Passengers:* 105 first plus 20 cots. With UMTATA (built 1935, sunk 1942) formed trio built for Natal Line (Bullard King & Co. Ltd.), service to South and Portuguese East Africa. In September 1940 UMGENI, like UMTATA, was severely damaged by blitz on London Docks. Bought by Elder Dempster Spring 1957.

TAMELE,* TARKWA

Route: Liverpool – Port Harcourt (via intermediate ports). *Built:* 1945 by Cammell Laird, 1944 by Caledon. *Tonnage:* 7,173/7,414 gross. 8,110/ 7,620 d.w. *Dimensions:* 451 ft × 59 ft. *Draught:* 26 ft 2 ins. 460 ft × 59 ft. *Draught:* 26 ft 1 in. *Engines:* Doxford/B. & W. type diesels. Twin screw. (TARKWA single screw.) *Speed:* 13¼ knots. *Passengers:* TAMELE: 36 first; TARKWA: 40 first, 32 third. The Company's war-time losses were particularly heavy, and included their three major passenger ships. Of the great rebuilding programme thus called for, TAMELE and TARKWA were the first to come into service.

ELDERS & FYFFES LTD., London ('Fyffes Line')

CAMITO*

Route: U.K. – Barbados, Trinidad, Jamaica – U.K. *Built:* 1956 by A. Stephen & Sons, Glasgow. *Tonnage:* 8,687 gross. 5,995 d.w. *Dimensions:* 448 ft × 62 ft. *Draught:* 26 ft 1 in. *Engines:* D.R. geared turbines. Twin screw. *Speed:* 17½ knots. *Passengers:* 103 plus 10 children (all first class). In design this ship is a virtual repeat of the GOLFITO. Passengers in single and two-berth cabins. Cargo space for 1,750 tons of bananas or 140,000 bunches.

ELDERS & FYFFES LTD., London ('Fyffes Line') (*contd.*)

GOLFITO*

Route: U.K. – Barbados, Trinidad, Jamaica – U.K. *Built:* 1949 by A. Stephen & Sons, Glasgow. *Tonnage:* 8,740 gross. 5,800 d.w. *Dimensions:* 447 ft × 62 ft. *Draught:* 26 ft 3 ins. *Engines:* D.R. geared turbines. Twin screw. *Speed:* 17½ knots. *Passengers:* 101 plus 10 children (all first class). Besides these two, the Company owns a number of other banana ships trading to the West Indies and the British Cameroons (W. Africa) which have accommodation for 10–12 passengers. U.K. terminal ports are Avonmouth, Liverpool (Garston Docks), and Southampton.

ELLERMAN & BUCKNALL LINE, London

CITY OF PORT ELIZABETH, CITY OF EXETER,* CITY OF YORK, CITY OF DURBAN

Route: Monthly to S. Africa (London, Las Palmas, Cape Town, Port Elizabeth, E. London, Durban, L. Marques and Beira). *Built:* 1952, 1953, 1953, 1954, by Vickers-Armstrongs, Newcastle. *Gross tonnage:* PORT ELIZABETH 13,363, others 13,345. *D.W. tonnage:* 11,350, 11,350, 11,406, 11,400. *Dimensions:* 541 ft × 71 ft. *Draught:* 28 ft 6 ins. *Engines:* Doxford type diesels. Twin screw. *Speed:* 16½ knots. *Passengers:* 107 first. The largest in the great Ellerman fleet, these ships are designed to make the passage from London to Cape Town in 16 days. The CITY OF PORT ELIZABETH, the first of the quartette, entered service in January 1953.

ELLERMAN'S WILSON LINE, LTD., Hull

BORODINO*

Route: Hull – Copenhagen – Aarhus – Hull (fortnightly). *Built:* 1950 by Aisa S.B. Co., Troon. *Tonnage:* 3,206 gross. 1,955 d.w. *Dimensions:* 312 ft × 49 ft. *Draught:* 18 ft. *Engines:* Trip. exp. and L.P. exhaust turbine. Single screw. *Speed:* 13½ knots. *Passengers:* 36 first. Of this very large fleet, the BORODINO is the only ship to carry over 12 passengers. She is specially designed to carry cargoes of dairy produce. So that she may claim the priority given to such perishable cargoes, she has a grey hull, in contrast to the Company's usual green.

FURNESS BERMUDA LINE (Furness Withy & Co. Ltd., London)

QUEEN OF BERMUDA*

Route: New York – Bermuda (weekly basis). Cruises: New York – Bermuda – Nassau – W. Indies. *Built:* 1933 by Vickers-Armstrongs, Barrow. *Tonnage:* 22,501 gross. 6,175 d.w. *Dimensions:* 579 ft × 77 ft. *Draught:* 27 ft 1 in. *Engines:* Turbo electric. Quad. screw. *Service speed:* 20 knots (18½ knots cruising). *Passengers:* 733. All public rooms air-conditioned. Every cabin has private bath and toilet. The only ocean liner besides QUEEN MARY to have three funnels. During the last war she served first as an A.M.C. and then as a transport. Released from Government since spring 1947. Her former sister, MONARCH OF BERMUDA, is now the Greek Line's ARKADIA.

OCEAN MONARCH*

Route: New York – Bermuda (weekly basis). Cruises: New York – Bermuda – Nassau – West Indies. *Built:* 1951 by Vickers-Armstrongs, Newcastle. *Tonnage:* 13,654 gross. 5,280 d.w. *Dimensions:* 516 ft × 72 ft. *Draught:* 24 ft. *Engines:* D.R. geared turbines. Twin screw. *Speed:* 18 knots. *Passengers:* 414. Fully air-conditioned. Launched on 27 July 1950, she made her maiden sailing from New York to Bermuda on 3 May 1951. Every cabin has private bath and toilet.

FURNESS WARREN LINE, Liverpool (Furness Withy & Co. Ltd.)

NEWFOUNDLAND,* NOVA SCOTIA

Route: Liverpool – Canada and U.S.A. (Liverpool, St John's, N.F., Halifax, N.S., Boston, Mass., and vice-versa). *Built:* 1948, 1947, by Vickers-Armstrongs, Newcastle. *Tonnage:* 7,437/7,438 gross. 6,562/6,550 d.w. *Dimensions:* 440 ft × 61 ft. *Draught:* 25 ft 6 ins. *Engines:* Geared turbines. (NOVA SCOTIA S.R.) Single screw. *Speed:* 15 knots. *Passengers:* 62 first, 92 tourist. Strengthened for ice. About one-fourth of total cargo space insulated. These two perpetuate the names of an earlier pair built 1925–26, which during the war served respectively as a hospital ship and troopship, until their loss by bombing and torpedo.

35

GLEN LINE LTD., London

BRECONSHIRE, GLENARTNEY, GLENEARN,★ GLENGYLE, GLEN-
ORCHY (ex Priam 1948)

Route: U.K. and Continent – Port Said, Malaya, Hong Kong, China,
Japan (and Ceylon homewards only). *Built:* 1942, 1940, 1938, 1940,
1941, by Caledon, Dundee. *Tonnage:* 9,061/8,992/8,960/8,957/9,324 gross.
Approx. 9,600 d.w. *Dimensions:* 507 ft × 66 ft. (GLENORCHY 513 ft.)
Draught: 30 ft 6 ins. *Engines:* B. & W. type diesels. Twin screw. *Speed:*
17 knots. *Passengers:* Up to 18, one class. These five ships, also the
following three, are of similar design. GLENORCHY first owned by Blue
Funnel Line. BRECONSHIRE similarly, laid down as TELEMACHUS – but
completed as escort carrier ACTIVITY; bought by Glen Line 1946 and
entered present service 1947.

DENBIGHSHIRE, GLENGARRY,★ GLENROY

Route: U.K. – Japan (see BRECONSHIRE for ports). *Built by:* 1. 1938,
Netherlands S.B. Co., Amsterdam. 2. 1940, Burmeister & Wain, Copenhagen. 3. 1938, Scotts, Greenock. *Tonnage:* 8,983/9,144/8,959 gross.
Approx. 9,600. *Dimensions:* 507 ft × 66 ft. *Draught:* 30 ft 7 ins. *Engines:*
B. & W. type diesels. Twin screw. *Speed:* 17 knots. *Passengers:* Up to 18,
one class. GLENGARRY seized by Germans while completing, became
commerce raider MEERSBERG and HANSA. Recaptured at Kiel 1945 and
given temporary EMPIRE (HUMBER) name. During war GLENEARN,
GLENGYLE, and GLENROY used by Admiralty first as Fleet Supply, then
as landing ships. GLENARTNEY and DENBIGHSHIRE, after surviving
several Malta convoys, formed part of the Pacific Fleet Train.

HENDERSON LINE (P. Henderson & Co., Glasgow)

PROME,★ SALWEEN

Route: U.K. – Burmese ports, via Port Said and Aden. *Built:* 1937, 1938,
by Denny, Dumbarton. *Tonnage:* 7,043, 7,063 gross. Both 9,400 d.w.
Dimensions: 462 ft × 59 ft. *Draught:* 27 ft 4 ins. *Engines:* S.R. geared
turbines. Single screw. *Speed:* 14 knots. *Passengers:* SALWEEN 76;
PROME 74. One class. The last passenger ships to be built for the Company before its acquisition by Elder Dempster Lines in 1952. Since then
most of their fleet – the rest are cargo ships – have been employed on the
W. African trade.

NEW ZEALAND SHIPPING CO. LTD., London

RANGITANE,* RANGITOTO

Route: London (embark passengers) Curacao, Panama Canal, New Zealand, Back by same route to Southampton (land passengers) and London. *Built:* 1949 by J. Brown; 1949 by Vickers-Armstrongs, Newcastle. *Tonnage:* 21,867/21,809 gross. 14,700/15,000 d.w. *Dimensions:* 609 ft × 81 ft. *Draught:* 32 ft 1 in. *Engines:* Doxford type diesels. Twin screw. *Speed:* 16½ knots. *Passengers:* 416 one class. RANGITOTO, the first of the pair, was launched in January 1949. The RANGITANE perpetuates the name of one of the Company's ships (a sister to the RANGITIKI) which was sunk in the Pacific, 26 November 1940, by a German raider.

RUAHINE*

Route: U.K. – New Zealand. Ports as RANGITANE above. *Built:* 1951 by J. Brown, Clydebank. *Tonnage:* 17,851 gross. 12,380 d.w. *Dimensions:* 584 ft × 75 ft. *Draught:* 29 ft 7 ins. *Engines:* Doxford type diesels. Twin screw. *Speed:* 16½ knots. *Passengers:* 267 one class. Slightly smaller than the pair above, the RUAHINE is the third of the Company's ships to be so named. The first, of 6,100 tons, was built in 1891. The second had a remarkably long and successful career. Built in 1909, with a tonnage of 10,800, she saw 40 year's service with the Company, then a further 8 years as the Italian-owned AURIGA before being scrapped.

RANGITATA,* RANGITIKI

Route: U.K. – New Zealand. Ports as RANGITANE. *Built:* 1929 by J. Brown, Clydebank. *Tonnage:* 16,969/16,985 gross. 12,948/12,748 d.w. *Dimensions:* 552 ft × 79 ft. *Draught:* 33 ft 8 ins. *Engines:* Doxford type diesels (fitted 1949 and 1948). Twin screw. *Speed:* 15½ knots. *Passengers:* RANGITATA: 123 first, 288 tourist; RANGITIKI: 121 first, 284 tourist. During war both used as transports, coming through unscathed. In November 1940 the RANGITIKI narrowly escaped falling victim to the Pocket Battleship ADMIRAL SCHEER, which had just sunk the famous JERVIS BAY and several others in the same convoy.

ORIENT LINE, London

ORIANA*

Route: U.K. – Australia, then from Sydney and Auckland on Orient & Pacific Lines' trans-Pacific service. *Built:* by Vickers-Armstrongs, Barrow. *Tonnage:* 40,000 gross. *Dimensions:* 804 ft × 97 ft. *Draught:* 31 ft 6 ins. *Engines:* D.R. geared turbines. Twin screw. *Speed:* 27 knots. *Passengers:* 600 first, 1,500 tourist. Stabilisers. Fully air-conditioned. Ordered 1956. Keel laid September 1957. Bow and stern thwartship propellers to aid manoeuvring. With ORSOVA, ORONSAY, ORCADES, and five of P. & O., will operate on joint Pacific service. In this Australia and N.Z., American W. Coast, and Japan form triangle.

ORSOVA*

Route: U.K. – Australia, then on Orient & Pacific Lines' trans-Pacific service. *Built:* 1954 by Vickers-Armstrongs, Barrow. *Tonnage:* 28,790 gross. 11,610 d.w. *Dimensions:* 723 ft × 90 ft. *Draught:* 30 ft 8 ins. *Engines:* Geared turbines. Twin screw. *Speed:* 21.8 knots. *Passengers:* 685 first, 813 tourist. Complete air-conditioning planned. Named after a past Orient Line favourite (in service 1907–36) and also small town by Danube 'Iron Gate' rapids. Launched on 14 May 1953, the same day as P. & O. ARCADIA. Left Tilbury on maiden voyage 17 May 1954. Owners' third post-war liner and the first ship of any size without conventional mast. Then the largest liner to have all-welded hull. Cost £6½ million.

ORONSAY*

Route: U.K. – Australia, then on Orient & Pacific Lines' trans-Pacific service. *Built:* 1951 by Vickers-Armstrongs, Barrow. *Tonnage:* 27,632 gross. 10,704 d.w. *Dimensions:* 709 ft × 90 ft. *Draught:* 30 ft 5 ins. *Engines:* Geared turbines. Twin screw. *Speed:* 21.8 knots. *Passengers:* 668 first, 833 tourist. Full air-conditioning to be fitted 1959. Maiden voyage 16 May 1951. Distinguished from earlier sister ORCADES by thick mast. On withdrawal of trans-Pacific liner AORANGI made experimental extended voyages 1954 to Auckland, Vancouver, and San Francisco, this leading to creation of Orient and Pacific Lines' service.

ORIENT LINE, London (*contd.*)

ORCADES*

Route: U.K. – Australia, then on Orient & Pacific Lines' trans-Pacific service. *Built:* 1948 by Vickers-Armstrongs, Barrow. *Tonnage:* 28,164 gross. 11,140 d.w. *Dimensions:* 709 ft × 90 ft. *Draught:* 30 ft 5 ins. *Engines:* Geared turbines. Twin screw. *Speed:* 21.8 knots. *Passengers:* 635 first, 742 tourist. Fully air-conditioned. The first of the Orient Line's post-war programme and a contemporary of the P. & O. Line's HIMA-LAYA, she was launched on 14 October 1947. Maiden voyage 14 December 1948. Cost £3½ million. Refitted and given air-conditioning early 1959.

ORION*

Route: U.K. – Australia (Tilbury, Gibraltar, Marseilles, Naples, Port Said, Aden, Colombo, Fremantle, Adelaide, Melbourne, and Sydney). *Built:* 1935 by Vickers-Armstrongs, Barrow. *Tonnage:* 23,696 gross. 11,200 d.w. *Dimensions:* 665 ft × 82 ft. *Draught:* 30 ft 2 ins. *Engines:* S.R. geared turbines. Twin screw. *Speed:* 19 knots. *Passengers:* 342 cabin or tourist, 722 tourist 'B'. Built at a cost of £920,000, the ORION entered service in September 1935. Noteworthy in being the first large liner to have only one mast and the first Orient ship to be permanently painted with buff hull. After war-time trooping she returned to commercial service in 1947.

ORONTES*

Route: U.K. – Australia. (For ports see ORION.) *Built:* 1929 by Vickers-Armstrongs, Barrow. *Tonnage:* 20,186 gross. 8,941 d.w. *Dimensions:* 664 ft × 75 ft. *Draught:* 30 ft 2 ins. *Engines:* S.R. geared turbines. Twin screw. *Speed:* 18 knots. *Passengers:* 1,410 one class. The last of five 20,000-tonners (others ORAMA, ORFORD, ORONSAY, and OTRANTO), she was launched in February and entered service October 1929. Built for £950,000, she had a £1 million refit after war-time trooping. She returned to service in June 1948. One class ship since 1953.

P. & O. LINE, London (Peninsular & Oriental S. Nav. Co.)

CANBERRA★

Route: U.K. – Australia, then on Orient and Pacific Lines' trans-Pacific service. *Built:* by Harland & Wolff, Belfast. *Tonnage:* 45,000 gross. *Dimensions:* 820 ft × 102 ft. *Draught:* 32 ft 6 ins. *Engines:* Turbo-electric, approx. 85,000 s.h.p. max. *Speed:* 27 knots. *Passengers:* 600 first, 1,650 tourist. Two sets of stabilisers. Fully air-conditioned. The most outstanding liner now building, her estimated cost is £15 million. Keel laid September 1957, nine days after future consort ORIANA. The Orient & Pacific Lines' triangular coverage of Pacific will be by 9 ships: CANBERRA, IBERIA, ARCADIA, HIMALAYA, CHUSAN, and four of Orient Line.

IBERIA★

Route: U.K. – Australia, then on Orient & Pacific Lines' trans-Pacific service. Also cruising. *Built:* 1954 by Harland & Wolff, Belfast. *Tonnage:* 29,614 gross. 10,056 d.w. *Dimensions:* 719 ft × 91 ft. *Draught:* 30 ft 5 ins. *Engines:* Geared turbines. Twin screw. *Speed:* 22 knots. *Passengers:* 673 first, 733 tourist. Stabilisers. Full air-conditioning planned. The last of 6 liners ordered for the Australian trade under Orient and P. & O. postwar building programme. Launched 21 January 1954. Averaged 24.9 knots on trial. Maiden voyage 28 September 1954. Sister to Clyde-built ARCADIA.

ARCADIA★

Route: U.K. – Australia, then on Orient & Pacific Lines' trans-Pacific service. Also cruising. *Built:* 1954 by J. Brown, Clydebank. *Tonnage:* 29,734 gross. 10,646 d.w. *Dimensions:* 721 ft × 91 ft. *Draught:* 31 ft. *Engines:* Geared turbines. Twin screw. *Speed:* 22 knots. *Passengers:* 675 first, 735 tourist. Stabilisers. Full air conditioning fitted 1959. The fourth P. & O. liner ever to be built on the Clyde, the ARCADIA was launched on 14 May 1953, the same day as the Orient Line's ORSOVA. Maiden voyage from Tilbury 22 February 1954. Reputed cost £6½ million. Named after a famous 6,000-ton P. & O. liner built 1888.

P. & O. LINE, London (Peninsular & Oriental S. Nav. Co.) (*contd.*)

HIMALAYA*

Route: U.K. – Australia, then on Orient & Pacific Lines' trans-Pacific service. Also cruising. *Built:* 1949 Vickers-Armstrongs, Barrow. *Tonnage:* 27,955 gross. 11,810 d.w. *Dimensions:* 709 ft × 91 ft. *Draught:* 31 ft. *Engines:* Geared turbines. Twin screw. *Speed:* 22 knots. *Passengers:* 758 first, 401 tourist. Stabilisers. Full air-conditioning to be fitted late 1959. Averaged 25.13 knots on trial. Maiden voyage October 1949. Then the largest and fastest P. & O. liner. Funnel top added 1953. Early 1958 opened new Pacific service, from Sydney and Auckland to North America. Left Sydney March 1959 (after voyage from U.K.) to inaugurate U.S. – Japan service, returning home via India.

CHUSAN*

Route: London – Far East, and on Orient & Pacific Lines' trans-Pacific service. Also cruising. *Built:* 1950 by Vickers-Armstrongs, Barrow. *Tonnage:* 24,215 gross. 9,860 d.w. *Dimensions:* 672 ft × 85 ft. *Draught:* 29 ft. *Engines:* Geared turbines. Twin screw. *Speed:* 22 knots. *Passengers:* 470 first, 522 tourist. Stabilisers. Full air-conditioning to be fitted at end 1959. The first large passenger ship to be fitted with Denny-Brown stabilisers. Safely launched 28 June 1949 despite accident when being waterborne. Tried June 1950. Made several cruises before first voyage to Bombay (in September) and first full length trip to Hong Kong November 1950.

CANTON*

Route: U.K. – Far East (Southampton/London, Port Said, Aden, Bombay, Colombo, Penang, Singapore, Hong Kong). *Built:* 1938 by A. Stephen, Glasgow. *Tonnage:* 16,033 gross. 10,080 d.w. *Dimensions:* 563 ft × 73 ft. *Draught:* 29 ft 6 ins. *Engines:* S.R. geared turbines. Twin screw. *Speed:* 18 knots. *Passengers:* 298 first, 244 tourist. The Company's third to bear this name and the last of their large passenger ships to be completed with a black hull, she entered service on 7 October 1938. Converted 1939 into an A.M.C. and used for escort duties. Later became a transport. Returned to Far Eastern service October 1947.

P. & O. LINE, London (Peninsular & Oriental S. Nav. Co.) (*contd.*)

STRATHEDEN*

Route: U.K. – Australia (London, Port Said, Aden, Bombay, Colombo, Adelaide, Fremantle, Melbourne, Sydney (Marseilles homewards only). *Built:* 1937 by Vickers-Armstrongs, Barrow. *Tonnage:* 23,732 gross. 11,000 d.w. *Dimensions:* 664 ft × 82 ft. *Draught:* 30 ft 2 ins. *Engines:* S.R.-geared turbines. Twin screw. *Speed:* 19 knots. *Passengers:* 529 first, 453 tourist. Launched in June 1937 and commissioned in December 1937, she and her later sister STRATHALLAN (sunk December 1942) were the last of the STRATHS to be built. After war-time trooping the STRATH-EDEN was the first P. & O. to return to service – in June 1947. In 1950 made four Cunard trips to New York.

STRATHMORE*

Route: U.K. – Australia (See STRATHEDEN for ports.) *Built:* 1935 by Vickers-Armstrongs, Barrow. *Tonnage:* 23,580 gross. 11,000 d.w. *Dimensions:* 665 ft × 82 ft. *Draught:* 30 ft 2 ins. *Engines:* S.R.-geared turbines. Twin screw. *Speed:* 19 knots. *Passengers:* 497 first, 487 tourist. The third of the STRATH series and the first to have only one funnel, she also had different type machinery. Launched by the Duchess of York (now the Queen Mother), she was delivered in September 1935. A war-time troopship, she took part in the N. African landings. Returned to peace-time service October 1949.

STRATHNAVER, STRATHAIRD*

Route: London – Australia. (See STRATHEDEN for ports.) *Built:* 1931, 1932, by Vickers-Armstrongs, Barrow. *Tonnage:* 22,270/22,568 gross. 8,783/9,050 d.w. *Dimensions:* 664 ft × 80 ft. *Draught:* 29 ft 2 ins. *Engines:* Turbo-electric. Twin screw. *Speed:* 17½ knots. *Passengers:* 1,252/1,242 one class. These, the first of the STRATHS, originally had three funnels, the two dummies being removed after the war. The STRATHNAVER spent nine years trooping and took part in the N. African landings. The STRATH-AIRD served for seven years as a transport, returning to commercial service in January 1948.

P. & O. LINE, London (Peninsular & Oriental S. Nav. Co.) (*contd.*)

CORFU, CARTHAGE*

Route: U.K. – Far East (Southampton/London, Port Said, Aden, Bombay, Colombo, Penang, Singapore, Hong Kong). *Built:* 1931 by A. Stephen, Glasgow. *Tonnage:* 14,280/14,283 gross. 10,210/10,420 d.w. *Dimensions:* 543 ft × 71 ft. *Draught:* 29 ft 9 ins. *Engines:* S.R.-geared turbines. Twin screw. *Speed:* 17½ knots. *Passengers:* 181 first, 213 tourist. The original intention was to name these two CHEFOO and CANTON. As built they had black hulls, two funnels, and a short well-deck forward. Both were used first as A.M.C.s and then as transports during the war.

Managed for Ministry of Transport

EMPIRE FOWEY* (ex Potsdam 1946)

Route: Government troop-carrying. *Built:* 1935 by Blohm & Voss, Hamburg. *Tonnage:* 19,116 gross. 7,040 d.w. *Dimensions:* 634 ft × 74 ft. *Draught:* 27 ft 2 ins. *Engines:* D.R.-geared turbines. Twin screw. *Speed:* 18 knots. *Passengers:* 153 first, 94 second, 92 third, 1,297 troops. New engines 1950. Built as one of a notable trio for N.D.L.'s express Far East service (others GNEISENAU and SCHARNHORST, both war losses). Given 2½-year reconstruction on Clyde 1947–50 when stripped to hull plating and old boilers and turbo-electric machinery removed. Now the last of our big ex-German troopships.

THE PACIFIC STEAM NAVIGATION CO.

REINA DEL MAR*

Route: Liverpool – Valparaiso, via France, Caribbean, W. Indies, Venezuela, Panama, Ecuador, Peru, Bolivia. *Built:* 1956 by Harland & Wolff, Belfast. *Tonnage:* 20,234 gross. 12,634 d.w. *Dimensions:* 601 ft × 78 ft. *Draught:* 30 ft 1 in. *Engines:* D.R.-geared turbines. Twin screw. *Speed:* 18 knots. *Passengers:* 207 first, 216 cabin, 343 tourist. Air-conditioned throughout. Stabilisers. This ship, delivered in March 1956, makes four round trips a year. She replaces the famous REINA DEL PACIFICO which, after 27 years' service, was scrapped at Newport, Mon., in 1958.

ROYAL MAIL LINES, LTD., London

ANDES*

Route: Cruising only. *Built:* 1939 by Harland & Wolff, Belfast. *Tonnage:* 25,676 gross. *Dimensions:* 669 ft × 83 ft. *Draught:* 29 ft 3 ins. *Engines:* S.R.-geared turbines. Twin screw. *Speed:* 21 knots. *Passengers:* Approx. 500 first. Stabilisers. Air-conditioning. After wartime trooping duties she was used in May 1945 to take the Norwegian Government back to Norway after its long exile. The largest British ship built for the South American service, she did not enter this until January 1948. After making many cruises, the ANDES, following a refit at Flushing during the winter of 1959/60 is to be used solely for this purpose.

AMAZON,* ARAGON, ARLANZA

Route: London, French ports, Vigo, Lisbon, Las Palmas, Recife or Salvador, Rio de Janeiro, Santos, Montevideo, Buenos Aires. *Builders:* Harland & Wolff, Belfast. *Tonnage:* Approx. 20,000 gross. *Dimensions:* 583 ft × 78 ft. *Draught:* 28 ft 9 ins. *Engines:* Harland & Wolff turbo-charged diesels. Twin screw. *Speed:* 17½ knots. *Passengers:* 107 first (15 interchangeable), 82 cabin (30 interchangeable), 275 third. Stabilisers. Fully air-conditioned. These three, designed to replace the HIGHLAND class, will cost a total of at least £15 million. Three permanent swimming pools. Every first-class cabin with bath or shower; many cabin class with showers. Third class 2, 3 or 4 berths only. AMAZON: Maiden voyage January 1960.

HIGHLAND BRIGADE, HIGHLAND MONARCH,* HIGHLAND
    PRINCESS

Route: London, Vigo, Leixoes, Lisbon, Las Palmas, Rio de Janeiro, Santos, Montevideo, Buenos Aires. *Built:* 1929, 1928, 1930, by Harland & Wolff, Belfast. *Tonnage:* all 14,216 gross and 8,811 d.w. *Dimensions:* 544 ft × 69 ft. *Draught:* 28 ft 8 ins. *Engines:* B. & W. type diesels. Twin screw. *Speed:* 15¼ knots. *Passengers:* 104 first, 335 third. These ships being replaced by Amazon class (above). HIGHLAND BRIGADE will be withdrawn from service in August 1959, PRINCESS in December, and MONARCH in 1960. Owned until 1932 by Nelson Line.

SHAW SAVILL LINE (Shaw Savill & Albion Co. Ltd., London)

SOUTHERN CROSS★

Route: Round the world either Westabout or Eastabout. Ports: Southampton, Trinidad, Curacao, Panama Canal, Fiji, Wellington, Sydney, Melbourne, Fremantle, Durban, Cape Town, Las Palmas, Southampton (or in reverse). *Built:* 1955 by Harland & Wolff, Belfast. *Tonnage:* 20,204 gross. No cargo. *Dimensions:* 604 ft × 78 ft. *Draught:* 25 ft 10 ins. *Engines:* D.R.-geared turbines. Twin screw. *Speed:* 20 knots. *Passengers:* 1,100 tourist. Stabilisers. Fully air-conditioned. The largest liner yet to have engines aft and the first trading to Australia and New Zealand to carry no cargo.

DOMINION MONARCH★

Route: U.K. – Australia and New Zealand, out and back via S. Africa (London, Southampton, Las Palmas, Cape Town, Fremantle, Melbourne, Sydney, Wellington). *Built:* 1939 by Swan Hunter & Wigham Richardson, Newcastle. *Tonnage:* 26,463 gross. 16,860 d.w. *Dimensions:* 682 ft × 85 ft. *Draught:* 34 ft 1 in. *Engines:* Doxford type diesels. Quad. screw. *Speed:* 19½ knots. *Passengers:* 508 first. When new the largest ship regularly trading to Australia and New Zealand. From August 1940 onwards was used as a transport. With the fall of Singapore she narrowly escaped becoming a Japanese prize, being in dry dock with engines dismantled. Returned to commercial service late 1948.

ATHENIC★ and CORINTHIC, CERAMIC and GOTHIC

Route: U.K. – New Zealand via Panama Canal out and back (London, Curacao, Panama, Auckland/Wellington). *Built:* 1947, Harland & Wolff, 1947; Cammell Laird, 1948; Cammell Laird, 1948; Swan Hunter. *Gross tonnage:* 15,187/15,682/15,896/15,911. *D.W. tonnage:* 11,658/11,365/11,390/11,530. *Dimensions:* First pair: 560 ft × 71 ft. *Draught:* 29 ft 8 ins. Others: 561 ft × 72 ft. Draught: 29 ft 7 ins. *Engines:* Geared turbines. (First two S.R.) Twin screw. *Speed:* 17 knots. *Passengers:* 85 first. Of these four ships which carry large amounts of refrigerated cargo the first, the CORINTHIC, entered service in April 1947. The latter pair – slightly more beamy – differ in having Thornycroft smoke-deflecting funnel tops. The GOTHIC was used for the Royal Tour of 1952.

UNION-CASTLE LINE, London

PENDENNIS CASTLE*

Route: Mail service. Southampton, Cape Town, Port Elizabeth, East London, Durban (also calls Las Palmas or Madeira). *Built:* 1958 by Harland & Wolff, Belfast. *Tonnage:* 28,582 gross. 15,600 d.w. *Dimensions:* 763 ft × 84 ft. *Draught:* 32 ft 2 ins. *Engines:* D.R.-geared turbines. Twin screw. *Speed:* 22 knots. *Passengers:* 197 first (includes 33 interchangeable = 66 tourist), 473 tourist. Partial air-conditioning. Stabilisers. Following the Clan/Union-Castle merger early in 1956, the ship, then newly laid down was lengthened by 16 ft. (to receive stabilisers) and given higher-powered machinery. The PENDENNIS CASTLE entered service 1 January 1959, replacing the ARUNDEL CASTLE.

PRETORIA CASTLE,* EDINBURGH CASTLE

Route: Mail service, Southampton – S. Africa (details as PENDENNIS CASTLE). *Built:* Both 1948 by Harland & Wolff. *Tonnage:* 28,705 gross. 16,688/16,558 d.w. *Dimensions:* 747 ft × 84 ft. *Draught:* 32 ft. *Engines:* D.R.-geared turbines. Twin screw. *Speed:* 22 knots. *Passengers:* 214 first, 541 tourist. Built as replacements for the WARWICK and WINDSOR CASTLES (war losses), both ships had notable launchings. The EDINBURGH CASTLE was christened by Princess Margaret, while the launching of the PRETORIA CASTLE was performed by Mrs. Smuts, by radio telephony, from Africa. The Company's first turbine driven mailships for nearly 30 years.

CAPETOWN CASTLE*

Route: Mail service, Southampton – S. Africa (details as PENDENNIS CASTLE). *Built:* 1938 by Harland & Wolff. *Tonnage:* 27,002 gross. 14,925 d.w. *Dimensions:* 734 ft × 82 ft. *Draught:* 32 ft. *Engines:* B. & W. type diesels. Twin screw. *Speed:* 20 knots. *Passengers:* 243 first, 553 tourist. The first CASTLE not to be named after a place in the British Isles. She was christened (September 1937) by Mrs. J. D. Low, Mayoress of Cape Town. The last and largest of the Company's mail ships to be diesel driven. Is still the longest motor liner in the world.

UNION-CASTLE LINE, London (*contd.*)

STIRLING CASTLE, ATHLONE CASTLE★

Route: Mail service. Southampton – Cape Town, Port Elizabeth, East London, Durban (also calls Madeira/Las Palmas). *Built:* 1936 by Harland & Wolff. *Tonnage:* 25,554/25,567 gross. 15,421/15,138 d.w. *Dimensions:* 725 ft × 82 ft. *Draught:* 32 ft. *Engines:* B. & W. type diesels. Twin screw. *Speed:* 20 knots. *Passengers:* 245 first, 538 tourist. ATHLONE CASTLE launched November 1935, was christened by Princess Alice, Countess of Athlone. During the war both ships were used as transports and from 1943 operated on the North Atlantic, bringing U.S. troops to Britain. Even after twenty years widely regarded as two of the most handsome motor liners ever built.

WINCHESTER CASTLE★

Route: Mail service. Southampton – S. Africa (details as STIRLING CASTLE). *Built:* 1930 by Harland & Wolff. *Tonnage:* 20,001 gross. 12,425 d.w. *Dimensions:* 657 ft × 75 ft. *Draught:* 32 ft 1 in. *Engines:* B. & W. type diesels (new 1938). Twin screw. *Speed:* 20 knots. *Passengers:* 188 first, 398 tourist. Originally two-funnelled. Of the five mail ships re-powered in the 'thirties, was the only one not lengthened. Thus now the only CASTLE with a vertical stem. In 1941–2 acted as a training ship for assault troops; later took part in landings in Madagascar, N. Africa, and Southern France.

CARNARVON CASTLE★

Route: Mail service, Southampton – S. Africa (details as STIRLING CASTLE). *Built:* 1926 by Harland & Wolff. *Tonnage:* 20,148 gross. 14,314 d.w. *Dimensions:* 686 ft × 73 ft. *Draught:* 32 ft 9 ins. *Engines:* B. & W. type diesels. Twin screw. *Speed:* 20 knots. *Passengers:* 134 first, 450 tourist. Built with two squat funnels and vertical stem, she made history as the Company's first motorship and the first Cape liner to exceed 20,000 tons. Lengthened and given more powerful engines 1938. In 1940, as an A.M.C., she intercepted and damaged German raider THOR. Later served as transport.

UNION-CASTLE LINE, London (*contd.*)

RHODESIA CASTLE, KENYA CASTLE, BRAEMAR CASTLE*

Route: London – round Africa. BRAEMAR out via W. Coast, other two out via Suez. *Built:* 1951, 1952, 1952, by Harland & Wolff. *Gross tonnage:* First two: 17,041, BRAEMAR 17,029. *D.W. tonnage:* 10,693/10,656/10,834. *Dimensions:* 576 ft × 74 ft. *Draught:* 28 ft 2 ins. *Engines:* D.R.-geared turbines. Twin screw. *Speed:* 17½ knots. *Passengers:* BRAEMAR: 552 cabin; others: 526 cabin. The commissioning of the third of this trio, the BRAEMAR CASTLE, late in 1952, was an occasion of special importance to the Company, for it also marked the completion of their post-war liner replacement programme.

BLOEMFONTEIN CASTLE*

Route: Intermediate service London – Beira via Cape (London, Rotterdam, Las Palmas, Walvis Bay, Cape Town, Port Elizabeth, E. London, Durban, L. Marques, Beira and back. Also Ascension and St Helena (outward only). *Built:* 1950 by Harland & Wolff. *Tonnage:* 18,400 gross. 10,750 d.w. *Dimensions:* 595 ft × 76 ft. *Draught:* 29 ft 1 in. *Engines:* B. & W. type diesels. Twin screw. *Speed:* 18½ knots. *Passengers:* 721 cabin. The Company's first one-class ship, she entered service in April 1950. Her maiden voyage was round Africa, but since then she has plied as above, via the West Coast. In January 1953, when off the Mozambique coast, she rescued the survivors from the wrecked KLIPFONTEIN.

DURBAN CASTLE,* WARWICK CASTLE (ex Pretoria Castle 1946)

Route: London – round Africa. DURBAN out via West Coast, WARWICK out via East Coast. *Built:* 1938, 1939, by Harland & Wolff. *Tonnage:* 17,382/17,387 gross. 10,802/10,590 d.w. *Dimensions:* 595 ft × 76 ft. *Draught:* 29 ft 2 ins. *Engines:* B. & W. type diesels. Twin screw. *Speed:* 18½ knots. *Passengers:* 180 first, 359 tourist. During the war the DURBAN CASTLE was used as a transport and landing ship. As the latter assisted at landings on N. Africa and Southern France. Her sister became first an armed merchant cruiser and then an aircraft carrier. From 1947 to 1950 both operated on the mail service until larger vessels became free.

UNION-CASTLE LINE, London (*contd.*)

WINDSOR CASTLE

38,000 tons gross. *Building:* by Cammell Laird. *Dimensions:* 783 ft × 92 ft. *Draught:* 32 ft. Geared turbines. Twin screw. *Speed:* 23 knots. Passengers: 250 first, 600 tourist. Fully air-conditioned. Stabilisers. Launched by the Queen Mother 23 June 1959. Maiden voyage due August 1960.

TRANSVAAL CASTLE

30–35,000 tons. *Building:* by John Brown, Clydebank. 800 passengers, one class.

ADDENDA

CAPTAIN COOK (page 28) on offer for new charter, summer 1959.

HIGHLAND BRIGADE and HIGHLAND PRINCESS (page 52). Sold Latsis Line, Athens, for new service to Australia and New Zealand. Will carry 900 one class passengers and 4,000 tons of refrigerated cargo.